Cost...
A-Pl...

Customize
Your Programs
with How-To Ideas
for School and
Beyond

By
**JANET
EDEWAARD**

HAL•LEONARD®

ISBN: 978-1-61780-783-1

Published by Hal Leonard Corporation
7777 W. Bluemound Road
P.O. Box 13819
Milwaukee, WI 53213

Library of Congress Cataloging-in-Publication Data

Edewaard, Janet.
  Costumes a-plenty : customize your programs with "how-to" ideas for school and beyond / by Janet Edewaard.
      p. cm.
  ISBN 978-1-61780-783-1
  1. Costume. 2. Handicraft. I. Title.
  TT633.E28 2011
  391--dc23
                                    2011019229

Printed in the U.S.A.

First Edition

Visit Hal Leonard Online at
www.halleonard.com

To my sisters, Connie and Cherie,
who still aren't too old to play dress up!

Table of Contents

Around the World 6

Bears 16

Birds 17

Circus Characters 19

Decorated Tee Shirts 22

Dinosaurs 25

Dogs 27

Fairy Tale Characters 32

Forest Animals 36

Historical Figures 38

Insects 40

Miscellaneous Costumes 44

Nuts 49

Through the Ages 50

Underwater Creatures 62

Introduction

By Janet Edewaard

I had the privilege of growing up on a farm in the rural panhandle of Florida. My parents raised grain, cattle and five "doorstep" children. We didn't have neighbors within walking distance, so my siblings were (and still are) my best friends. We spent our days making villages out of the freshly bailed hay and "fairy castles" down at the creek, when we weren't picking blackberries, peas or shucking corn. It was a wonderful childhood! My parents were (and still are) very loving and encouraged us to be creative. We didn't have a lot of expensive toys, but my sisters and I had the best costume collection imaginable! We would play for hours in old prom dresses and could create what we needed out of bits and pieces of old clothing. When all the costumes were created, we would put on elaborate "plays". (The hearth on our fireplace was our stage.) Our two brothers had to sit and watch our productions.

As we got older, Mom taught us to be excellent seamstresses and I started sewing all my clothes. As we grew up and got married, we passed that creativity on to our children. When I became a teacher, all four of my children were in school. Costumes and creativity were so engrained in my life that it spilled over in my classroom. From half-time shows to musicals, costumes became the trademark of my teaching. I taught my daughters to sew by making costumes for my school productions.

After several years of teaching, I met John Jacobson and he asked for some costume suggestions for a musical he was writing called *Bugz!* Knowing that sewing is a vanishing art, I offered costume suggestions that required little or no sewing. After *Bugz* came the musical *Circus, Circus* and my partnership with John was born! It's been over ten years and I continue to write costume suggestions for several of his musicals each year. You don't have to be a seamstress to follow my instructions. Just as "duct tape can fix anything", a trip to a secondhand store and a hot glue gun can create almost any costume. Happy creating!

Costumes from Around the World

The African Continent

African-printed fabric can be purchased at most fabric shops, but it's usually quite expensive. Consider using just a small piece as an accent. The basic African costume is a caftan, which can be made very inexpensively. Take a flat sheet and fold it in half. Cut a slit at the fold, large enough for the person's head to go through. With the fabric still folded, leave an opening 10" – 12" from the fold and sew the sides together. This leaves an opening for the arm. Do the same thing on the other side. It will look like a giant pillowcase with openings in the top and sides. From there you can add colorful accents of the expensive fabric, by wrapping it around the body, or head. Use your imagination. To make the costumes look a little more regionally correct, use the following suggestions.

Here is a picture of the cast from my production of *The Elephant's Child* by John Jacobson and Emily Crocker. The basic caftan was used in every costume. To that, large colorful African fabrics were draped (and pinned in place) to add color and character. Tempera paint enhanced their characters. (front) Snake; (center) Kola Kola Bird, Elephant Child, Crocodile; (back) Narrator.

Egypt: Black caftan for girl with black veil to cover her face. Only her eyes should show. For the boy, a stripped caftan, floor length.

Ethiopia: Solid white, baggy pants and a large white sheet draped around shoulders and torso.

Kenya: Bright orange fabric. Make a floor length wrap-around skirt, and tie same fabric around the girl's torso. Add a large circular collar out of gold wrapping paper. For boy, wrap orange fabric around body for a short toga.

Sudan: Beige fabrics wrapped around body.

Tanzania, Rwanda, Burundi: Bright colorful fabrics wrapped around body. Use matching fabric wrapped around head.

Uganda: Wrap several different colors of fabric around the child. Make a cape for over-the-shoulders. Add a colorful scarf for headdress.

Zaire: Striped fabric tied around girl like a sarong; make it floor length. Use the same fabric to wrap head.

Australia

The bush men wore long khaki trousers, with a long buttoned shirt. If you can borrow a pair of leather boots, great! Instead of an expensive leather bush hat, use a straw hat. Then with a needle and thread, string fishing corks around the brim of the hat. The bush men did this to keep flies away. Tie a bandana around the neck and you are ready to go "Down Under"!

Brazil

In some areas of Brazil, the women wear long skirts, bright, colorful blouse, and lots of bead necklaces and bracelets. To obtain the appropriate materials, go to a secondhand store. Look for women's skirts that are full and will reach the floor on a child. Choose a solid color tee shirt that is color coordinated with the skirt and will fit the child. Purchase crepe-paper streamers in various colors from your favorite discount store. Cut streamers in 3-foot lengths. Then, using a needle and thread, make long stitches, in and out, along the length of one side of the streamer. When you get to the end, pull the thread and gather up the streamer. Tie a knot and hold it in place. Do this again with the other streamers. Loosely sew a ruffled streamer over each sleeve of the tee shirt. Add bead necklaces and bracelets and you will have a Brazilian costume! If you want an extra touch of flavor, add a headpiece with fruit and flowers. This can be made with plastic fruit, silk flowers, a handle-less basket, and a hot glue gun. Glue the fruit and flowers in the basket, glue the basket to a scarf, and tie it around the girl's head.

What works well for a boy's Brazilian costume are baggy pants and a poncho. Again, a thrift store will have all the baggy pants you require. Buy men's pants and cut them off 2" longer than you need. You can purchase iron-on hemming tape and "hem" the pants to the correct length. (The hemming tape will allow you to use them again after they have been washed.) You will need a belt to hold the pants up, but the poncho will hide the belt. To make the poncho, buy inexpensive fabric with a woven design. This can easily be found at a discount store. One yard should be enough for each poncho. Simply fold the fabric in half and cut a slit in the center for the head to go through. If you can find a gaucho hat and boots, your costume will be complete!

Germany

For the German boy or man, you need a pair of black shorts and a short-sleeved white button up shirt with a red neck tie. The shorts need to be knee length. If you can't find any the correct length, go to a secondhand store and buy a pair of dress pants and cut them off two inches longer than they need to be. Using iron-on hemming tape, hem them to the correct length. You need to purchase a multicolored braid, preferably a black background with several colors woven in it. It needs to be long enough to go from the waist over the shoulder twice and add about 8" to it. Safety pin the braid on the underside of the waistband of the shorts, to make suspenders. Then cut a piece long enough to go between the two suspenders on the front. (You want it to look like a "H".) Safety pin that so the pin doesn't show. Buy some over-the-calf tube socks and a pair of black dress shoes. The hat will be hard to purchase. You can make one by purchasing a yard of green felt. Remember how you would fold a newspaper into a hat? Well, do the same thing with the green felt and hot glue it in place. Add a red ribbon and you have the German hat! (The reason you want to use felt is that the ends won't fray and the felt has enough body to hold its shape.)

For the German woman, you need a skirt that is "candle length" which means it is about six inches off the floor. The skirt should be very full. You need a white long-sleeved blouse and a black vest that is waist length. This should be a corset type vest that laces up in the front. Add a solid color apron in the front. Make sure it is a contrasting color to the skirt. You need one yard of a floral fabric to fold in half in a triangle and tie around the shoulders. Check at a secondhand store for a black hat with a wide brim. Add a white ribbon on the brow and hot glue a flower on the back.

Hawaii

The people of Hawaii often wear loose, brightly colored clothing. The "aloha shirt" (commonly called a Hawaiian shirt) is a sport shirt with brightly colored tropical designs. If you are on a tight budget, you might need to be a little creative. The boys can simply wear shorts and solid bright-colored shirts.

For the girls, you must first require them to wear a swimsuit under their costume. Take a piece of fabric two yards long. Tropical prints would be wonderful, but they are expensive. If each girl has a different brightly colored fabric, the effect will be stunning. Discount stores that sell fabrics usually have a bargain table. Have the girl hold her arms up, and then wrap the fabric around her by doing the following: Center it on her back, bring it to the front, crisscross it and tie the ends around her neck.

Add leis and/or shell necklaces, and you have it made! Both can be purchase in most party supply stores. Or, you can be creative and let the students make their own leis. Supplies you will need include:
- bright colors of construction paper
- plastic drinking straws
- yarn and tape
- hole punch
- scissors

Cut 2-inch circles out of the construction paper. Scallop the edges. Using a hole punch, punch a hole in the center. Cut drinking straws into 1-inch lengths. Cut the yarn into one-yard pieces. String the flowers and the straws, alternating circle, straw, circle, straw, etc. (If you wrap a piece of tape around the end of the yarn, it will keep the yarn from fraying.) Tie the ends together when finished.

Korea

On a limited teacher's budget, a look of traditional Korean clothing can be achieved by visiting a secondhand store. Look for women's skirts that have a gathered waist and are quite full. (It doesn't matter if it's too big.) The skirt should hang well below the child's knees. Add a contrasting, long-sleeved blouse, preferably a V-neck, and the costume is complete. A crew-neck white tee shirt should be worn under the V-neck blouse so that it can be seen peeking out from the blouse at the neckline. Take the skirt and pin it to fit the girl just under her breast, as this is the way the women's traditional clothes are worn. If possible, pull hair back in a tight bun – with enough hair spray and bobby-pins, almost any length of hair will go into a bun!

For the boys, have them bring a pair of extra-large jogging pants (maybe from their fathers or older brothers). It is ideal if the pants are too long, as the men's traditional pants are very loose and baggy and bunch up at the feet. A large bathrobe that hangs below the knees should be tied at the breast. Again, traditional Korean costumes do not tie around the waist, but below the breast.

Netherlands

The women wore long skirts, with a white blouse and a white apron. Add a shawl to drape around the shoulders. Make sure you use some stripes in this costume. The Dutch loved stripes! There are many different ways to make a Dutch hat. The hats were made from lace or stiff white fabric. Some of the pictures are similar to the bonnets worn in the early Americas. Use your imagination. Make sure there are some high peaks and long hanging ribbons on the hat. Now, the easy part, the Dutch shoe! With Crocs being so popular today, just add a pair of Crocs and you are set!

The men wore wide woolen pants with silver buttons on the front square flap. If you don't want to completely sew a pair of Dutch pants, take this tip. Go to a secondhand store and buy a pair of men's pants in a basic color. Take the pants to a fabric store and try to match the fabric as much as possible. Buy ¼ yard of this fabric. While you are there, buy four silver buttons. Cut out a rectangle of this fabric and sew a button on each corner. Safety pin this (with the pins on the back side) to the front of the dress pants. Cut the pants off 2" longer than you need and hem them with iron-on hemming tape. A simple dress shirt and a basic jacket will go with this. The hats were different with every region, but a close-fitting hat would work just fine.

Scotland

It is doubtful that you will find a kilt in a secondhand store. Wool plaid fabric is very expensive and you will need several yards to make a kilt. So, here's how I make an inexpensive kilt. Buy three yards of plaid flannel fabric. Fabric is normally 45" wide. You won't need it to be that long. Measure the person from the waist to the knee cap. Add four inches to that measurement. Cut away the extra fabric and save it to make the beret. Two inches of this will be the hem. Press down a half inch of the long side to keep the kilt from fraying when it is washed. Turn up 1.5 inches of the wrong side of the kilt and use iron-on hemming tape to hem the kilt. You will be folding the three yards of fabric into pleats. Play with the fabric to see how wide your pleats need to be and how close together. It will vary from the size of the person. You need to make it wide enough so that when it is completely pleated, it will wrap all around the person and overlap about 10 inches. Once you determine your pleats, steam-iron them in place. Press the entire piece of fabric into pleats, much like a paper fan. Take the edge of the kilt that has not been hemmed and press it under two inches. Use hemming tape to keep this in place. The top will be pressed solid. The bottom will not be, so the pleats can open up. Wrap the kilt around the person, starting on the front pelvic area and wrap completely around the body and over to the other pelvic area. Make marks where this is and then hot glue Velcro into the overlapped area to hold it up. With a needle and thread, sew four large brass buttons down the outside of the overlap. There is your kilt!

Add a white dress shirt and a men's jacket. Borrow some Boy Scout socks if you know someone in the Scouts. If not, you will need to go to a Celtic online store to purchase socks. They are not cheap. The cheapest pair I found was about $12.00 but you have to have the tall, over the knee socks to complete the outfit. You can either purchase a beret or make one from the leftover fabric.

Sweden

According to legend, Sweden once suffered a great winter famine. At the height of the famine, a ship of peaceful Vikings sailed across Lake Vannern, bearing food for the Swedes. At the helm was a beautiful young girl, Lucia, dressed in white and wearing a glowing halo. Now, on December 13, the youngest daughter of each house commemorates Lucia by wearing a crown of candles on her head and a long white robe. The other daughters wear long white robes and wreaths of evergreen on their heads. The girls go to each room to wake their sleeping family and serve them coffee and saffron buns. In more modern traditions, the boys are included and wear white robes and pointed paper hats with golden stars.

To make a "Lucia," choose your smallest girl and dress her in white and make a crown of candles for her head. To make a crown, get a green Styrofoam wreath (available in the floral supply section of a discount store), punch holes in the wreath large enough for five battery operated candles, and cover the wreath with evergreen. Dress the other girls in white robes and make wreaths of evergreen for their hair. You can include the boys by dressing them in white robes and making pointed paper hats for them. Glue a few golden stars onto the hats.

Thailand

Thailand is the country where *The King and I* was written in. In the movie, it was referred to as Burma but it is modern day Thailand.

Here is how I outfitted my cast for that production.

For the men, I took two yards of fabric and made something that looks like a diaper. Turn the fabric where it is longer than wider and tie the top around his waist, with the tie facing the back. Then pull the fabric between his legs and bring it up to the back side and tie in the front. Ask your men to wear some shorts underneath this in case the sides gape open. No shirt is needed. If your men are uncomfortable showing their chests, make an overlay for them. Measure from the shoulders to waist and double the measurement. Add 6" to that measurement. Take a piece of contrasting fabric and fold in half. Cut a slit along the fold, large enough for his head to fit through. Hot glue a 12-inch ribbon on each side (that will be a total of four ribbons). Tie these in place and his chest is not seen. No shoes are necessary.

For the women, take a piece of fabric between two and three yards long. Fold the fabric in half. Have them wear a swimsuit underneath this for modesty. Have her raise her arms and place the fold under her arm, running down one side. Crisscross the fabrics to the other side and tie above her shoulder. No shoes are necessary either. Large jewelry and hair braided up and out of the way present well.

The "diaper" directions are given. The tunics were purchased at a secondhand store. I added colorful sashes that were cut 6" long using 45-inch wide fabric. I sewed two of them together to make a long sash. The cone hats, from Oriental Trader, cost about a dollar each.

Here is the simple wrap that I give directions to make. Some of the wraps were expensive fabrics and others were from bed sheets I bought at a secondhand store. If you put just a few nice fabrics on stage, you can get by with humbler fabrics for the majority of the girls.

Here is a close up of the wrap-around dress. I added an expensive drape of fabric to hide the cheap fabric I used for her dress. I purchased her snake arm band at an online theatrical site. Madi Gras beads are braided into her hair.

For the children, purchase long-sleeved tee shirts. (You can find them online very reasonably and in every color of the rainbow.) Make the same "diaper" that the men wore but you will have to adjust the length, due to the various heights of your children. The tee shirt will tuck in the diaper. To make a chocker for the child, purchase 2-inch wide gold and black braid (look online for good prices) and cut it 3" longer than the width of the child's neck. Hot glue Velcro on the ends and you have a chocker! To make the child's crown, go to a carpet supply store and ask for one of the tubes that carpet comes wrapped around. Have someone cut the tubes into 4-inch lengths and spray paint them gold. Using the same gold and black braid that you used for the chocker, hot glue the braid on the center of tube. Next, take a measurement from ear to ear running under the child's chin and add two inches. Cut black quarter-inch elastic and glue on the inside of the crown. This will hold the crown on the top of the child's head. Have the girls put their hair in a bun that sits on top of the head. (The boys in Burma had short hair.) If you wanted to go all out, purchase black hair spray (available online at a theatrical supply company) and spray each child's hair black before you put the crown on. It comes out with shampoo. The added touch would be to require each child to use a sunless tanning product or get a spray on tan. (Brace yourself, if you do this, you won't recognize your own kids!) The Royal Children don't need shoes.

Directions are given for making the children's costumes. I purchased long-sleeved tee shirts online and then used contrasting colors to make their "diapers". The crowns are made from a carpet tube, as explained above. I had the kids use black hairspray and spray-on tans.

Wales

Think "Mother Goose" for this costume. She needs a long solid-colored skirt and a long color coordinated blouse. A black vest needs to be short or either tucked in the skirt. Take ½ yard of very colorful fabric and drape it over her shoulders and pin it in the front. Now for the most important part, she needs a black witch hat that you have altered. The hat needs to be flat on the top but must be taller than a man's top hat. Take the witch hat and cut it off at the point that the diameter is 5". Take black poster board and cut a five inch circle. Carefully place this circle into the top of the hat and very carefully, hot glue it in place.

15

Bears

THE BASICS

Start with a basic sweat suit, and go from there! For their heads, you could use either "doo-rags" or headbands. Cheap white doo-rags can be purchased online, then dye them to match the colors you need, and hot glue small felt ears to the top. Another idea would be to purchase plastic headbands and glue the felt ears to the band. You may want to also paint a big brown nose on each bear or whatever color the costume is.

SPECIALTIES

Featured in
*A Bear-y
Merry Holiday*
Musical by
John Jacobson & John Higgins

Black Bears: Black sweat suits.

Dancing Bears: Dancing Bears need to be brown. Poll your cast and see what type of "Dancing Bears" they would like to be. Cowboy hats and red bandanas around their necks would make adorable "Country Line Dancing Bears". If you have a good bit of budding ballerinas, tutus would be precious over their sweats. (They would have them from a dance recital.) If you want "Hip-Hop" dancing bears, put them in saggy shorts and oversized tee shirts over their sweats.

Grizzly Bears and Kodiak Bears: Brown sweats.

Panda Bears: They need white spots added to their black sweat suits. Oriental Trader has inexpensive cone-shaped Asian straw hats that would be perfect for each Panda to wear. Just glue ears on the outside of the straw hat, and they're set to go!

Polar Bears: White sweats.

Teddy Bears: Have some fun with these and go with every color of the rainbow! Then cut out a big circle in a contrasting color and hot glue on their tummy.

Birds

THE BASICS

For bird costumes, have every child get a pair of tights. Color will depend on type of bird. Purchase packages of colored feathers (at craft shops) and plastic hair bands. Glue feathers on the hair band to give each bird character.

Body & Legs

Here are two different ways to create the body of a bird. Girls could wear a leotard with yellow tights. These can be purchased online. Since birds are small, use your smallest girls who won't mind being in something that is so form-fitting. A pair of shorts or a short skirt can be added for modesty. Bird legs are skinny (and from someone who has been called "bird legs" her entire life, let those little girls show off their skinny little legs!)

Another way to create the body of a bird is to use a small white garbage bag with a drawstring. Cut openings in the bottom of the bag for the child's legs, and openings in the sides for the child's arms. Then stuff newspaper between the child and the garbage bag. Pull the drawstring up around the child's neck to secure it.

Wings

One way to make wings would be out of the appropriate colored poster board and then glue feathers on the very edge of the wing. Hot glue elastic on the underside of the poster board to hold the wings on the child's arms.

The other way to make wings would be to take one yard of a matching color chiffon fabric and gather it down the middle. Attach a loop of elastic to one end of each side, so the child can put it on their wrist. Attach the gathered section to the back of the costume.

Face

Face painting will add a special touch to these costumes. Paint the face the same color as the costume; add a yellow beak and accent the eyes.

SPECIALTIES

Bluebird: Blue leotard with a blue ballerina tutu.

Chicken and Rooster: Red tights.

Duck: White tights. Cut large fan-shaped feet out of orange poster board. At the small end, cut an opening for the child's ankle. Punch holes on either side of the opening and lace a ribbon through the holes so you can tie the cardboard foot on, at the child's ankle.

Goose: Use a taller child than the duck. The costumes could be identical, except a different color. White tights are needed.

Owl: Yellow tights and a brown leotard. Add brown wings. Paint the child's face brown and with yellow circles around the eyes.

Penguin: White sweat suit and black socks. Take a large black trash bag and cut down one side seam. Place the point of the uncut corner on the child's head. Take a yard of 1-inch black satin ribbon and tie around the child's neck and around the garbage bag to make a bow tie. This will hold the "hood" on the child's head. Have the child hold their arms slightly out and trim the plastic bag to make a flipper to cover their white arms. Using a clear package tape, secure the flipper to the underside of the child's arm. A little yellow makeup around the eyes would set these penguins off!

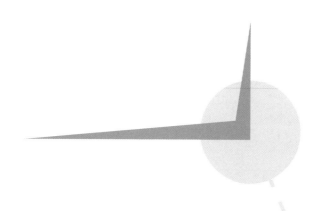

Circus Characters

Ringmaster

Ask your school band director for the jacket to an old band uniform. Add a pair of dress pants and an old band hat. By the way, those old plumes on some band hats make great head dresses for circus girls!

Featured in
Circus Circus
Musical by
John Jacobson
& John Higgins

Circus Girls

Recruit the girls who have participated in pageants and let them put on their prettiest dress and tiara. Let others pull them around in a wagon as part of the circus parade. If they can get out and do some acrobatics, all the better!

Clowns

Every sewing pattern book has clown patterns in the costume section. If you aren't fortunate enough to have a super-mom who sews, a visit to the local secondhand store will provide you most of what you need. One idea is to take a pair of large adult pants and cut the legs to an appropriate length. A small hula hoop can be cut and run through the belt loops. Duct-tape it back together, after you have cut some of the width out of it. Suspenders are needed to hold up the pants. Add a large colorful shirt and a bowtie that clashes to complete the outfit. Find a pair of men's XL shoes and spray paint them a bright color. Stuff the toes with poly-fill and have the child put on the big shoes with his/her personal shoes inside. Clown wigs can be purchased inexpensively, or look for a wig at a secondhand store and spray paint it a bright color. If you don't have clown makeup, liquid tempera paint can be applied to the face and washed off easier than greasy stage makeup.

Dancing Bears

Brown sweat suits. Buy birthday party hats (the pointed ones) and hot glue brown felt ears on the hats. The elastic on the hat will hold the hat in place. Each bear could hold an inflatable beach ball and pretend to dance on the ball.

Elephants

Plain gray sweat suits. Long trunks can be made from cardboard tubes, vacuum cleaner hoses or clothes dryer hoses. Big floppy ears are a must! Make the ears out of gray felt and hot glue them to a gray "doo-rag". Long thin tails can be cut out of the felt and pinned on the back side of the sweat pants. Connect a line of "elephants" together in the circus parade by having them hold onto the tail of the elephant in front of them.

Flame Swallower

This one might be a bit more challenging to access the supplies needed. If you do have access to a cotton candy machine, purchase some orange cotton candy mix. Take a 1-inch wooden dowel and cut the length to 24 inches. Spin a little orange cotton candy on the end of the dowel. When it is time for the flame swallower to perform, have him come out and dramatically wave the "torch" in the air. Have him put the torch (of cotton candy) in his mouth and watch it magically disappears! Tah dah! Tah dah!

Lions

Golden yellow sweat suit, or buy a white sweat suit and dye it. Purchase a Styrofoam floral wreath big enough for the child's face to fit in, and wrap the ring with golden yarn. Create "pom-poms" to attach to the ring. Start by cutting a piece of heavy cardboard 4"x6". Wrap the yarn around the cardboard about 50 times. Then run a piece of yarn through one end and tie it off; slip it off the cardboard, and cut the looped end of the yarn. Tie pom-pom to front of Styrofoam ring. Make enough pom-poms to cover front of ring. Attach ¼" elastic to the backside to hold it to the child's head.

Lion Tamer

A pair of dark dress pants and a white shirt, tucked in, will do. A black top hat is a "must." If possible, add a coat with tails. He needs to carry a small whip (not to really use) and a small chair.

Strong Person

Stuff the shirt and pants of a sweat suit with polyfill to look like huge muscles. Have him/her flex muscles and pump barbells that are really Styrofoam on the ends of a broom handle. The bigger the muscles, the better!

Stunt People

Have some of the boys or girls wear shorts and tee shirts and ride their battery-operated "motorcycles" in a follow-the-leader pattern.

Sword Swallower

Take an inexpensive plastic sword with a hollow core and cut off the sword where it joins the handle. Stick a lump of play dough in the top of the handle. Push the sword about an inch into the play dough to hold it in place. When the sword swallower is ready to dazzle the audience, have him hold the sword up to his mouth, open his mouth wide and without closing his lips on the sword, bite the end of the sword. Slowly push the handle down over the sword to make it look like he's swallowing the sword. The trick is that the sword has gone into the handle. When it will go no further, have him extend both arms straight out, keeping his teeth clenched on the sword. Then, slowly pull the handle up until it's near the end of the sword. Tah dah! Tah dah!

Tight Rope Walkers

Dress the tight rope walkers in either leotards like a gymnast or a wrestler wears, or a one-piece swimsuit for the girls with white tights underneath. To make a headdress, purchase a bag of assorted feathers and a bag of assorted "jewels" from a craft store. Glue a cluster of feathers and jewels to the sides of a plastic head band. Add a parasol for balance for the girls. You can simply place an eight-foot long 2'x4' board on a set of cement blocks to simulate a tight rope. A balance beam from the gymnasium would do the trick as well. Make sure to have plenty of matting in case of an unplanned tumble!

Trapeze Artists and Tumblers

A few small swings on stage would be pretty ambitious but impressive. Add some monkey rings, too! Although most adult circuses don't make a big thing out of somersaults, a tumbling mat that allows your cast to show off their best round off, cartwheels and yes, somersaults, would be great!

Vendors

These are great for adding to the circus atmosphere! Have them wear aprons around their waists, like the nail aprons from the hardware store (you might get free), and carry popcorn in boxes from the local movie theatre. Cotton candy can be simulated by taking polyfill and wrapping it around a paper cone. Use a little hot glue to hold it in place. You can purchase floral spray paint from a craft shop and lightly spray the polyfill with pink or blue floral paint. To hold a bouquet of cotton candy, this vendor could have a big circle of cardboard with holes cut in it and the points of the cone stuck into it.

Decorated Tee Shirts

Getting Started

From time to time, you may find the need to design and decorate tee shirts. I teach swimming lessons every summer and my daughters crank out about 100 of them. Every summer we change the design and the kids love them! I have students who come for several summers and when they wear their tee shirts from a prior summer, I am pleased to see how well they hold up.

Maybe your class is doing a program where you want everyone to be dressed the same without going through a lot of expense. Maybe you are involved in a sporting event where you want everyone to wear the same thing. Maybe your child is having a party and you want a souvenir for everyone to take home. Remember the quote: "Been there, done that, bought the tee shirt!"

If you are doing a lot of shirts, you want to start with the most inexpensive tee shirt, which would be white. At many discount stores, you can purchase packs of five a lot cheaper than packs of three. The tee shirts dye real well. Simply follow the dyeing directions on the package.

Create Design and Pattern Pieces

You will need to create your design before you start. With swimming lessons, we buy primary coloring books and look for simple cartoon drawings of fish. These are easy to duplicate or simply trace. Large designs with a few details lend themselves well to tee shirts. Whatever your design, make sure it will fit in an 8½" by 11" block. Color the design on white paper to decide what colors you want.

Now, you need to transfer the design onto poster board, which will be strong enough to trace around. Every part of the design must be cut out separately. You might want to label each part. Take these to the fabric store because you will have to determine how much fabric to buy. Cotton fabric normally is 45" wide. You can have it cut to measure, but typically 1/8 of a yard is as small as they will cut. You have to decide how much fabric you need for the pieces you have cut. If you are incorporating a stripe, you might need extra fabric.

Pick Out Fabric

Take the colored design to a fabric store and try to find fabrics to make the design with. The cotton fabrics in the quilt section work real well because there is literally every color in the rainbow and the patterns are small enough to work on the small pieces of your design. For every part of the drawing, you will need a different fabric. For instance, if I was creating a fish, the body of the fish would be one print of fabric. The dorsal fin would be another print of fabric, the pectoral fin another fabric, the eye would be white and I would buy a large sequin type acrylic "jewel" for the colored part of the eye. (Remember, these are to be cute, not realistic.) You will find these in the craft section of a discount store.

Choose Fabric Paint

You also need to purchase several colors of fabric paint. These are in the craft section of a discount store. Make sure you have bought a color for every fabric you are going to use. I buy the four ounce bottles. They will do a lot of shirts and if you put the lids back on them, they will last a long time. Go ahead and buy a bottle of the silver glitter fabric paint. It makes a nice embellishment to any design. That's what we glue the eyes on the fish with. We also make water bubbles and swirls around the fish to look like the fish is underwater. It dries clear so all you see is the silver glitter.

Fabric Backing

The most important item you must buy to decorate the tee shirts is a product called "Wonder Under" or "Heat and Bond". It comes in five-yard packages, or you can buy it by the yard. It makes an iron-on transfer out of any fabric you buy. You can buy it at any craft store or fabric store. Decide how much you need for a specific shape and cut a piece. With a very hot iron, iron the Heat and Bond to the BACK SIDE of the fabric. Press for about 10 seconds. If you use cotton fabric, you don't have to worry about melting the fabric. Go on to the next color, till all the fabrics have Heat and Bond pressed on the back side. Now, trace the pattern on to the paper side of the Heat and Bond. With sharp scissors, carefully cut out the design.

Pull the paper backing (Heat and Bond) off the fabric and place on the tee shirt. Lay the entire design out on the tee shirt before you iron it down. For instance, if I was creating a fish, I would put the body of the fish down, and then add the fins, the stripes and the white eye. When you are happy with the placement, carefully steam-iron the design for about 10 seconds. It should be secure.

Finishing

Allow the shirt to cool. Slip wax paper inside the shirt to keep any paint from going through to the back side of the shirt. Carefully outline the fabric edges with the fabric paint so the ends won't unravel. Make sure the paint is halfway on the fabric and halfway on the tee shirt. Start at the top of the design and work your way down, careful not to smudge what you have already painted. It takes several hours for it to dry. After it is dry, you will come back and add embellishment, such as jewel eyes or lettering on the tee shirt.

Don't wash the shirt for 24 hours. If done well, the shirt will last for several years.

Dinosaurs

THE BASICS

The basic design for the dinosaur costumes will be a sweat suit and a baseball cap. If someone is handy with a needle and a thread, make tails for each dinosaur. Felt is sold by squares or by the yard. If you use felt for the tails, the ends will not fray, which eliminates part of the work. Make the tail three feet long. At the top, make it as large as the child's thigh. Taper it to two inches in diameter at the bottom. Stuff the tail with "polyfill," and then either sew it on the back of the sweat pants or simply safety pin the tail in place.

Some experts think that dinosaurs, like many modern birds and reptiles, were colorful animals. Some kinds of dinosaurs perhaps attracted mates by displaying brightly colored body parts. For example, a duckbill's head crest and a Ceratopsian's neck frill may have been vividly colored and served to attract mates. Whatever colors you choose, remember this: the more colors on stage, the bigger impact the entire production will be!

A baseball cap will be worn to the front on certain dinosaurs and to the back on others. It will serve as the base to attach teeth, plates, horns, feathers, etc… to the costume.

SPECIALTIES

Ceratopsians: Get creative with this costume. Add many feathers to the head. Fold colorful tissue paper into fans and hot glue them under the band of the hat to make it look like neck frills.

Featured in
Dinostars
Musical by
John Jacobson
& Mark Brymer

Diplodocus: This was the tallest of the dinosaurs. Make sure to give this role to that kid in your class that stands a foot taller than anyone else.

Hadrosaurus and Anatosaurus: These are the duck-billed dinosaurs. Use your imagination to make the hats as colorful as possible. Hot glue many brightly colored feathers to the hat. Turn the baseball cap to the front and pull way down over the child's eyes.

Micropachycephalosaurus: The translation for this dinosaur is "tiny thick-headed reptile." As in the Diplodocus where you chose the tallest children for this role, now choose your smallest children to play this character. If you could find some cheap, used bicycle helmets, paint them in a color that will coordinate with the sweat suit. Remember, tiny thick-headed reptile!

Pterodactyls: These flying prehistoric reptiles were not dinosaurs, but were closely related. These winged creatures are a *must* in your production! Take the child's sweatshirt and measure the length of the arm to the bottom of the waist. In other words, if the child were to raise his arms, how long would it be from the cuff of his shirt to the bottom band of the sweat shirt. Using that length, cut a circle out of felt with that measurement as the diameter of the circle. Cut the circle in half and these are the wings. Sew the straight side of this half circle to the sweatshirt, starting at the cuff and continuing to the bottom band of the sweatshirt, or hot glue in place. If you hot glue, keep in mind that this little fellow is going to flap his wings a lot, so make sure it is secure. Turn the baseball cap backwards and hot glue some more felt over the bib of the hat to make it longer and more pointed.

Raptors: These were fierce meat-eaters. Some of them might have flown. Make their costume similar to the T-Rex.

Stegasaurus: Take a green sweat suit and a green baseball cap. Cut 10 arrowhead-shaped plates out of orange foam sheets and hot glue one to the top of the hat and glue the others down the back. Make a tail out of green fabric. Add four floral cones at the end of the tail to be the four spikes at the bottom of the tail.

Triceratops: Floral shops have Styrofoam cones. Take three cones and paint them with a floral paint (or wrap with fabric) to match the sweat suit. Attach one "horn" to the bill of the hat and two on the crown of the hat. Turn the hat to the front.

Tyrannosaurus Rex: The books imply that he was green, but it's your choice. Take the baseball cap, turned to the front, and cut out jagged teeth out of white felt and hot glue on the bill of the hat.

Dogs

THE BASICS

The basic costume for each of the dogs could be a sweat suit and a "doo-rag" to cover each child's head and to attach the ears. You can go online and find them very reasonable - $12.00 for a dozen. I would buy brown, tan, black and white. The white ones can be dyed a color to match a specific costume. You will need matching colors of felt for the ears that can be attached with hot glue. Tails can be made with the same felt, and pinned on with a large safety pin. (Felt can be purchased by the yard or in 8"x11" rectangles.) White "over-the-calf" tube socks will be needed for some of the dogs. Pull the socks over the sweat pants to make the dog look like he has white legs and feet. Buy several colors of "duct-tape" to add spots on several of the dogs. If you cannot find the correct color sweat suit, buy white and dye it the desired color. If you cannot find theatrical makeup, tempera paint works well.

SPECIALTIES

Afghan: A tan sweat suit and a long blonde wig. Attach the long ears to a headband (no doo rag).

Featured in
ARF
Musical by
John Jacobson
& John Higgins

Bassett Hound: A brown sweat suit with white socks pulled over his pants. He needs VERY LONG ears. Use eye makeup to make his eyes look even bigger.

27

Beagle: A dark brown sweat suit. Pull a black tee shirt over the sweatshirt and white socks over his pants. Attach long floppy ears to his doo-rag.

Boxer: Brown sweat pants and a white sweatshirt. Add white socks over the pants. Buy plaid boxers to put over the sweat pants.

Chihuahua: Your smallest child. Tan sweat suit with a white tee shirt pulled over the shirt. Short ears attached to a sombrero (no doo rag.)

Chow: Put one of your biggest kids in a black sweat suit with a black doo-rag and short black felt ears (slightly rounded on the ends). For an extra furry look, purchase a Styrofoam floral ring big enough for the child's face to fit in. Wrap the ring with black yarn. Create "pom-poms" to attach to ring. Start by cutting a piece of heavy cardboard 4"x6". Wrap the yarn around the cardboard about 50 times. Then run a piece of yarn through one end and tie it off, slip it off the cardboard, and cut the looped end of the yarn. Tie the pom-pom to the front of the Styrofoam ring. Make enough pom-poms to cover the front of the ring. Attach ¼" elastic to the back-side of the ring, to hold it to the child's head. Make a big fluffy tail out of the leftover black yarn.

Dachshund: A medium brown sweat suit with medium droopy ears.

Dalmation: White sweat suit with black spots cut out of black duct-tape. Add a red ribbon around the neck.

Doberman: A black sweat suit with brown socks over the pants. He needs a brown doo-rag with black pointed ears.

English Bulldog: Tan sweat pants and a white sweatshirt. Find a British flag and attach to the front of his shirt. He needs medium floppy ears attached to his tan doo-rag.

German Shepherd: A brown sweat suit with a black tee shirt pulled over the shirt. He needs tall pointed ears on his doo-rag.

Irish Setter: A red sweat suit, red doo-rag and long shaggy ears. Take the red felt and cut many thin strips into the bottom edge of the ears, to make him look shaggy.

Labrador: A black sweat suit and a black doo-rag with medium black ears. Find a stuffed bird to hang around his neck.

Mixed Breed: Should look unkept and mismatched. Mabye brown pants and a grey sweatshirt. Add irregular splotches in brown and black duct tape to his suit. Make his face multi-colored with face paint. On his doo-rag, make his ears different lengths. See photo on page 31.

Pointer: A white sweatshirt and black sweat pants. Add black spots on her white shirt. She needs long ears attached to a doo-rag or headband.

Pomeranian: A tan sweat suit and a cheap short blonde wig. Take the wig and brush it over and over, till it's nothing but a fuzzy mess. Cut a small portion of the wig and glue it to the end of her tail. Glue short tan ears to a headband. (No doo-rag.)

Poodle: A white sweat suit and white doo-rag. Take a bag of cotton balls and hot glue all over the doo-rag. Glue cotton balls on her white ears too. Add a bow in her hair for a finish. A pair of white leg warmers would be adorable over her sweat pants. For a more elaborate touch, attach bunches of tulle fabric to ends of ears and top of head.

Retriever: A golden brown sweat suit with a matching doo-rag. Glue medium length golden ears to his doo-rag. Paint his nose brown.

Rottweiler: A black sweat suit with brown socks pulled over his pants. He needs a brown doo-rag with black ears. Dark brown face paint would complete his outfit.

Saint Bernard: Your biggest child. He needs a white sweat suit with a brown tee shirt pulled over. Find a small keg and tie it around his neck. Attach medium-length ears to his doo-rag or headband.

Schnauzer: A grey sweat suit with white socks over the pants. He needs a grey doo-rag with short pointed ears.

Shar Pei: A tan sweat suit that is way too big for him. (The bigger the better.) He needs a tan doo-rag with medium ears.

Shih Tzu: A long white wig (no doo-rag) with a ponytail up on the top of her head and a pink bow. She needs a gray sweat suit.

Siberian Husky: A grey sweat suit with white socks pulled over the pants. Add medium pointy ears to his grey doo-rag. This should be one of your "huskier" kids.

Terrier: A brown sweat suit with a black tee shirt pulled over the sweatshirt. Short floppy ears added to the doo-rag and a short black tail.

Fairy Tale Characters

Cat With a Fiddle

Use a black or gray sweat suit. Cut ears out of felt and stuff. See Billy Goats Gruff (page 35) for mounting ears on a headband. Use an eyeliner pencil to draw whiskers on the face. Add a cheap fiddle and you are set!

Chicken Little

Cut two pieces of poster board to resemble "wings." Cut out scallops of construction paper that resemble feathers and glue "feathers" on topside of wings. On the bottom, attach elastic to make a loop for the child's arm to hold the wings in place. Take a brown plastic trash bag and cut a hole for the child's head and two holes for the arms. Stuff with newspaper. Have the child wear a pair of orange tights. Take another plastic trash bag and cut two holes for the legs. Have child step through the holes and stuff with newspaper, then secure the bag around the waist using masking tape. Bring the top bag over the bottom bag and secure at waist. For head dress, glue feathers on a plastic headband. Use orange lipstick and paint the child's nose to resemble a beak.

Jiminy Cricket

Use a green sweat suit. With green poster board, cut out large wings. Punch holes in the wings and attach quarter-inch black elastic to hold the wings on. Jiminy must have a top hat. Add a plaid jacket and a bow tie. Paint his face bright green with bright yellow eyes and a big red mouth. Use tempera paint, if you cannot find face paint. It washes off easily.

Detail of face painting for Jiminy Cricket. Tempera paint was used.

Cinderella

Any long (pageant-style) dress will do for Cinderella. Add a tiara and dress shoes covered with silver glitter.

Humpty Dumpty

Take two white large garbage bags and cut two holes for arms and one hole for head. Place on child and stuff with newspaper. Take another bag and cut two holes for legs, stuffing with newspaper. (Have the child wear a pair of colored tights.) Pull the bottom bag over the top bag and secure with tape. Add a bolero style jacket (which will hide the tape on the bags). Add a paper collar, a big bowtie for the neck, and a hat ... and watch him fall!

Jack (from the Beanstalk)

Convince the young lad that all lads wore tights in the era that Jack was causing trouble in. A man's dress shirt (from a secondhand store) will be long enough to make a tunic for Jack. Cut off the collar of the shirt, leaving only the collar band. Find a small man's vest and put it over the tunic. Belt the tunic with a rope; add black dress shoes or ankle boots.

Jack and the Beanstalk's Mother

She needs a drab floor-length skirt and a ruffled white blouse. Add a "Martha Washington" hat and an apron.

Little Bo Peep

A frilly dress with pantaloons; a large bow in her hair and shepherd's hook.

Little Boy Blue

Blue knickers and a white shirt with suspenders. Blue socks and a trumpet will complete this outfit.

Little Miss Muffet

Below-the-knee, frilly dress and white pantaloons, with hair curled into ringlets.

Little Miss Muffet's Spider

The spider can be achieved in one of two ways. 1. Have Miss Muffet sit in front of a screen, so someone can drop a large stuffed toy spider on a fishing pole down behind the screen. Backlight the screen. 2. Have a child come out in a spider costume. Start with a black sweat suit. Take six black socks and stuff with polyfill. Sew three socks on the side seam of the sweat suit and the other three on the other side With a needle and thread, run fishing line through the end of the bottom "leg" and tie a knot on the top of the sock, making the fishing line secure. Go through the next leg and tie a knot at the top and bottom of the sock, leaving about four inches between the two legs. Go through the top sock and again, leave a 4-inch space, and secure it with fishing line. Take the fishing line and tie it to the underside of the sleeve of the sweat suit.

Little Red Riding Hood

A red dress with a red cape. Don't forget a basket of goodies. The cape could be as simple as a one yard piece of red fabric, draped over her shoulders and tied around her neck.

Mother Goose

A long flowing dress with an apron, a white wig and glasses.

Old Woman Who Lived in a Shoe

I would put her in a plain long dress, with apron. Attach baby dolls all over the dress and apron. Add a "Martha Washington" cap to her outfit.

Pinocchio

Small boy (or a girl) dressed in a collarless button down shirt, a vest and knee-length shorts. Add knee socks with ankle boots and a newspaper boy hat. With brown tempera paint, paint "joints" on his face, elbows and knees. Paint his eyebrows brown and bright red cheeks. Add a few brown dots to look like pegs holding him together. Purchase a latex "Pinocchio" nose from a theatrical supply with an elastic string to hold in place.

Detail of face painting for Pinocchio. I purchased the nose through an online theatrical site.

Here are Pinocchio and Jiminy Cricket. The cricket's sweat suit was a dull green. Pinocchio's shoes and hat were found at a secondhand store.

Rapunzel
A Medieval-style dress and long blonde wig. (Check party supply store.)

Rooster
Use the same idea as Chicken Little, only add long pieces of green, blue and orange construction paper to resemble tail feathers.

Sleeping Beauty
Similar to Cinderella but have her carry a ruffled pillow on stage, something only a princess would sleep with!

Three Billy Goats Gruff
Dye white sweat suits any shade of brown. Make horns out of felt, stuff with polyfill and attach to plastic headband. To make the horns stand up, use ice cream pushup pops. After you've eaten the ice cream, hot glue the flat part of the disk to the headband. Place the stuffed felt horn over the stick and it will make the horns stand up. Hot glue the horn around the plastic stick.

Three Little Pigs
Use pink sweat suits with pink painted faces. With an eyeliner pencil, draw a round circle around the nose and outline the child's nostril, or you can go online to a theatrical website and order pig noses to be attached to the face with liquid latex. You can also add clothes over the sweat suit to give personality. For example; shorts and suspenders on the boys and short frilly dresses on the girls.

Forest Animals

THE BASICS

Start with a basic white sweat suit. Dye the sweat suits according to the color you want. You will need several colors of floral spray (an aerosol spray paint florists use to color real and silk flowers). The spray can be purchased at craft stores. You will also need quilt batting, poly-fil and spray adhesive. These can be purchased at any craft store. You will also need assorted colors of felt. The basic headdress for each animal costume will be a "doo-rag." They can be found online very inexpensively and can be dyed to match the sweat suit. Ears should be cut out of felt and hot glued on to the doo-rag. Face painting is a *must*. So many of the animals will look like kids in sweat suits, unless you add face paint. You can purchase real "face paint" or, I find that tempera paint works just as well. Get a couple of moms to help paint faces before the show. The paint comes off easily with baby wipes.

SPECIALTIES

Badger: Gray sweat suit. Paint the child's face gray with a white strip down the nose and sides of the face. Add short black ears to the doo-rag.

Bat: Brown sweat suit and short ears on doo-rag. The bat will need wings. Take the child's sweat shirt and measure the length of the arm to the bottom of the waist. Have child raise his arm, and measure the distance from the cuff of shirt to the bottom band of the sweat shirt. Using that length, cut a circle out of felt with that measurement as the diameter of the circle. Cut the circle in half and these are the wings! Sew the straight side of this half circle to the sweat shirt, starting at the cuff and continuing to the bottom band of the sweatshirt, or hot glue in pace. If you hot glue, remember this little fellow is going to flap his wings a lot, so make sure it is secure.

Bear: Brown sweat suit. He doesn't need a tail. Add ears to his doo-rag. Paint his face black with a large tan area around his nose and mouth.

Bobcat: Tan sweat suit with very sharp pointed ears. Give him some cat whiskers. No tail.

Chipmunk: Brown sweat suit with a long brown tail. Short rounded ears. White eyes on a brown face.

Deer: Brown sweat suit. Short ears and a short white tail.

Fox: Rust (or red) sweat suit. The foxtail can be made from a long rectangle of rust (or red) poster board, covered with polyfill and sprayed rust (or red). Add ears to his doo-rag. Paint on a brown nose.

Mice: Gray sweat suit. Put large circular ears on the doo-rag with a pink insert in the ears. Add a pink nose and whiskers to the mice. Add a long pink tail out of felt, stuffed with poly-fill.

Opossums: Gray sweat suit, white face. The opossum needs a long skinny pink tail out of felt.

Porcupine: Gray sweat suit. Take gray pipe cleaners; cut in half. Punch sets of two small holes, quarter of an inch apart, all over the sweat shirt. Stick the cut pipe cleaner in one hole and out the other, and then twist it together where it comes out of the shirt to secure. This can be done all over the shirt. These pipe cleaners will be the quills. Add hair band with ears.

Rabbit: Since so many of the animals are gray and brown, put the rabbit in a white sweat suit for contrast. A simple tuft of polyfill will be adequate for the rabbit's tail. Use long bunny ears and put an insert of pink in the ears. The face needs to have a pink nose and whiskers.

Raccoon: Gray sweat suit. Make a tail similar to the squirrel tail but paint it black and gray. Short rounded ears on doo-rag. White face with black eyes, painted like a "Zorro" make.

Skunk: Black sweat suit. Make a tail similar to the squirrel but paint the outside black. Leave the center white. (Polyfill is white.) On the doo-rag, have short rounded ears. Hot glue a piece of white felt on the top of the doo-rag. Cut a piece of white felt to run down the back of the costume.

Squirrel: Gray sweat suit. Cut a long oval out of gray poster board. Using spray adhesive, cover both sides of the oval with polyfill. Using gray floral spray, paint the tail gray. Attach to the seat of the sweat pants, with the oval pointing up. Add small gray ears on the hair band.

Woodchuck (ground hog): Tan sweat suit, tan face, small ears.

Historical Figures in the Study of the Solar System

THE BASICS

Here are some basic costume-creating ideas:

- Suits can be purchased at secondhand stores for very reasonable prices.

- Knickers can be made from pants that are too short. Just cut them off at knee length.

- For Tsiolkovsky's collarless shirt, buy a white shirt at a secondhand store and literally cut off the collar. There is a collar band on every dress shirt. Leave the collar band on. If you wash it BEFORE you make the alterations on it, the shirt will be clean for the student. If you wash it afterwards, it will unravel and will be ruined.

- For beards, you can buy crepe beards from any theatrical supply online. If you are on a tight budget, get white cotton balls and Elmer's glue. Put glue on the parts of the face and stretch out the cotton balls. It makes a great white beard! You can color the beard with eye shadow if you don't want a snow white beard.

- Caftans can be made very simply. Take a couple of yards of fabric, fold in half, cut a hole for the neck and pin or loosely sew the sides. Leave a hole for the hands.

HISTORIC FIGURES

Featured in
Spaced Out
Musical by
John Jacobson
& Cristi Cary Miller

Aristotle: Gown with drape across the shoulders, short beard.

Copernicus: Black shirt with sleeveless red tunic over. Black knickers, black tights and slippers. A woman's wig (chin-length with bangs).

Einstein: Wild crazy white wig, big white moustache, crew neck sweater with white collar sticking out at neckline.

Robert Frost: Suit with white shirt and tie.

Galileo Galilei: Black knee-length dress, with long sleeves and a Puritan-type white collar, black tights and black ballet slippers, long white beard and moustache, with short black hair.

Hipparchus: Long caftan with a headband around his brow.

President Kennedy: Nice suit and tie.

Isaac Newton: Long white powder wig, black coat, white ascot tied around neck, black knickers, black tights and black slippers.

Sally Ride: Royal blue jumpsuit or royal blue sweat suit. Sew an American flag patch (can be purchased at craft stores) on the left shoulder. Attach several different patches on the front of suit.

Will Rogers: Cowboy hat, red bandana tied around his neck, western shirt and jeans.

Carl Sagan: Sports jacket and turtleneck sweater.

Tsiolkovsky: Glasses without legs (string attached), white goatee and moustache, collarless shite shirt and dark trousers.

Planets, Sun and Moon: Make large cut-outs of cardboard. Add rays coming off the sun (typical symbol of sun for students). Punch small holes in cardboard and tie elastic loops. This will give the students a way to hold the planet up. Have the students research which planet should be which color, what planets are larger and smaller, etc… Paint the cardboard. For Saturn, add cardboard rings to attach onto the planet.

Insects

THE BASICS

The basic insect costume should be a sweat suit. If you can't find the color you need, you can buy white sweat suits and dye them whatever color you need. Every "Bug" should have a pair of giant sunglasses. Type "giant sunglasses" on the internet and several sites will pop up. The cheapest price was $1.00 a pair. Most of the "Bugs" should have a pair of antennas. These can be made inexpensively with a plastic headband, pipe cleaners and two small Styrofoam balls placed on the end of the pipe cleaner (away from the head band.) You can purchase floral spray paint that will not melt the Styrofoam. Color coordinate the pipe clearness and the painted Styrofoam ball. I will state when antennas are not needed in certain costumes.

SPECIALTIES

Featured in
Bugz & A Bugz Christmas
Musical by
John Jacobson & John Higgins

Army Ants: Black sweat suit. Over the sweats, put Military fatigues. Add Army helmets, etc.

Asian Beetle: Looks a lot like a ladybug but is rust-colored instead of red. Cut large black spots out of felt and hot glue on costumes. Oriental Trader has the straw Asian hats for about $1.00 each. The antennas should stick out of the Asian hat.

Beetles: Refer to the soldier beetles, but add long-haired wigs and horn-rimmed glasses on one of them.

Boll Weevil: Brown sweat suit. Add cowboy hats with their antennas sticking out from the hat. Glue cotton balls at random on the hat.

Bumblebee: Black sweat suit. Get some yellow duct tape and wrap around the body.

Caterpillars that change into Butterflies: This may be the most challenging costume as they have to change right in front of the audience from caterpillars to butterflies. Perhaps giving them beautiful wings that are fastened underneath their arms and to the middle of their back so when they raise their arms they have wings. Then you could wrap them completely, with their arms at their sides in white gauze or cheese cloth. When the time comes for the change, others in the cast could help unwrap them in front of everyone until they are able to free their arms and raise their "wings."

Cockroaches: Black sweat suit. Add sombreros and a blanket over the shoulder.

Cricket: Black sweat suit. Refer to how the grasshoppers hold their arms.

Dragonfly: This insect should be very colorful. Attach a long tail out of felt and stuff it to the backside of the pants.

Flea: Black sweat suit, no antennas. Instruct the fleas to constantly be jumping around and itching themselves.

Fruit Fly: Needs a bright green sweat suit. Glue tropical fruit on the headband between the antennas. Put a tropical shirt over the sweat suit.

Glowworm: White sweat suit. Take a tee shirt and spray paint it florescent orange. It will be too stiff to put on the child. Cut the back side of the shirt and glue Velcro on the back to fasten it. No antennas needed.

Grasshopper: Green sweat suit with green antlers. Grasshoppers should always keep their elbows out with their hands on their hips, to look like legs sticking out.

Grub Worm: A tan sweat suit. Have him carry a small shovel and a bucket. Some garden gloves would be great! His face needs to be dirty.

Hornet: Brown top, black bottoms with yellow duct tape stripes.

Housefly: Black sweat suit. Put an apron on each fly, bedroom slippers and a shower cap. No antennas needed.

Ladybug: Red sweat suit with large black circles out of felt. Between the antennas, hot glue a big red bow on the hair band.

Lightning Bug: Bright yellow sweat suit. Give each lightning bug a flashlight to blink off and on.

Maggot: A white sweat suit with yellowish, white gauze wrapped around the child's torso. Make sure the child's face is dirty.

Monarch Butterfly: Black sweat suit. Buy a yard of orange chiffon and gather it down the middle. Attach the gathered section to the back of the sweat suit. Safety pin a loop of black quarter-inch elastic on the top edge of the sides. This will go over the child's wrists, to hold the wings in place. Encourage the child to flap their wings a lot! A tiara would really add the finishing touch!

Mosquito: Black sweat suit. Instead of antennas, get a foam floral cone and spray paint it black. Hot glue that on the headband.

Praying Mantis: Bright green sweat suit. Over the sweat suit, incorporate some sort of clerical wardrobe. Put a large cross around his neck. Instruct him to constantly bring the cross up to his lips to kiss.

Queen Bee: Refer to the bumblebees, but add a crown and a royal robe for the queen.

Soldier Beetle: Brown sweat suit. Put a camouflage jacket on each beetle.

Spider: A black sweat suit is needed and six black socks. Stuff the socks with polyfill. Sew three socks on the side seam of the sweat suit and the other three on the other side. With a needle and thread, run fishing line through the end of the bottom "leg" and tie a knot on the top of the sock, making the fishing line secure. Go through the next leg and tie a knot at the top and bottom of the sock, leaving about four inches between the two legs. Go through the top sock and again, leave a 4-inch space, and secure it with fishing line. Take the fishing line and tie it to the underside of the sleeve of the sweat suit.

Stink Bug: He needs an icky green sweat suit. His face should be dirty and his hair messy. Hang a braid of garlic around his neck.

Termite: Light tan sweat suit. Stuff their tops with pillows to make them look fat!

Yellow Jacket: Yellow top and black bottom with yellow duct tape around bottom half of costume.

Wood Tick: Grey sweat suit. Make sure the sweat suit is a good bit bigger than the child needs. No antennas are needed on the tick. Have the tick(s) start out skinny at the beginning of the show. Mid-way through the show, have them quietly exit the stage. Have someone back stage put in a pillow under the front and back of the shirt and pants. Near the end of the show, have them quietly exit the stage again and have someone place two more pillows under the suit. It will make them look like they are about to explode!

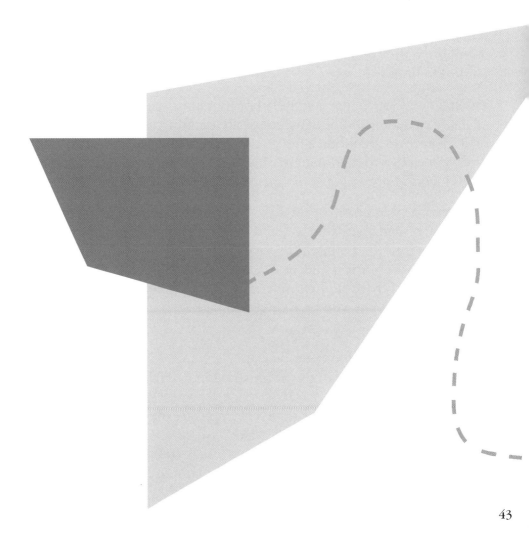

Miscellaneous Costumes

Child of the World

We all share the same air and walk the same earth, whether we come from the North, South, East or West. You could use the colors of the Olympic rings to represent world unity. The modern Olympics were organized to encourage world peace and friendship, as well as to promote amateur athletics. The games' symbol consists of five interlocking rings that represent the continents of Africa, Asia, Australia, Europe, and North and South America. The rings are black, blue, green, red and yellow.

Dress the children in white shorts and solid color tee shirts using the five colors of the Olympic symbol. (The white shorts will draw more attention to the colors of the tee shirts.) Have the children make a large circle and hold hands.

For an added touch, use five hula hoops, with each hoop painted one of the five Olympic colors. The hoops are then held by five small circles of students instead of one large circle. (This is especially effective if the boys don't want to hold the girls' hands, or visa versa. Each student can hold the hoop instead of someone else's hand.)

Flowers (that grow on stage)

Take a large garbage can and paint it a terra-cotta color. Make sure it is large enough for a student to squat down in. This will serve as your flower pot. Dress the child in a green sweat shirt and green gloves (accomplished by dyeing white cotton gloves green.) If the trash can is the correct height, you won't need to worry about a costume below the child's waist.

Purchase bright colors of crepe paper streamers (since you want to create beautiful flowers out of your children!). Take a 10" Styrofoam wreath and cover with a crepe paper streamer by wrapping the streamer around it. Using the same color, cut streamers in 3 feet lengths. Then, using a needle and thread, make long stitches, in and out, along the length of one side of the streamer. When you get to the end, pull the thread and gather up the streamer. Tie a knot to hold it in place. Hot glue the ruffle to the wreath. Do it as many times as you think makes a very full flower. Attach elastic to the back side of the wreath and this will hold the "flower" on the child's head.

Have the child squat in the painted garbage can. At the appropriate time, have her slowly lift her arms up, and slowly stand up with her head down. Then have her raise her head slowly to show what a beautiful flower she is!

Heroes

Just as our nation has heroes, every community has its own local heroes. This could lend itself very well to an interdisciplinary unit. Classroom teachers can help here by introducing heroes in the classroom. Poll the class to find out who they think are great American heroes. Then lead the children to discuss local everyday heroes they know. Is there a member in your community that has all the qualities of a hero? Maybe the school janitor is a hero (mine sure is!)

Let the class come up with about 10 different local heroes, then dress up selected students to look like them (tastefully, of course!) A wig and glasses can make a little girl look like the elderly sweetheart of the community. A bald cap (purchased at an online theatrical supply store) will make a statement if one of your heroes is lacking hair. For the performance, have each costumed child hold a sign bearing the hero's name.

Be sure to invite your local heroes to the performance!

May Day

May Day has been historically celebrated as a spring festival in many countries. People decorated their homes with spring flowers, sang spring carols, and gave gifts. Many towns chose a King and Queen of May. People danced around the May Pole which was decorated with bright ribbons.

When I was a child, my school celebrated May Day every year. The girls were asked to wear white dresses with bright colored sashes. The boys wore white shirts and dark dress pants. A bright colored sash was tied to each boy's waist. Once assembled "boy-girl-boy-girl" in a circle around the pole, all the girls faced one way and the boys faced the other. We then began skipping around the May Pole, weaving our colored ribbons around the pole.

Native American

Measure from the child's shoulder to their knees. Double this measurement and add two inches. Buy this amount of rough burlap. Fold in half and cut a "V" shape in the center of the fold. This should be wide enough for the child's head to go through. Unravel the bottom edges of the cut fabric, making two inches of fringe on the bottom of each edge. To unravel, simply pull the threads that run horizontally with the weave. On the inside, hot glue the sides together, leaving 10 inches for the arms. Hot glue braid or trim around the "V" neckline. Make a headband out of colorful braid. Hot glue some colorful quill shaped feather. (Purchase them at any craft store.) Safety pin it on the back to keep it securely in place on the child's head.

President Abraham Lincoln

Purchase a pair of black dress pants and a black jacket at a secondhand store. Give "Abe" a white dress shirt. Buying a top hat is much easier than trying to create one out of poster board. Party supply stores carry inexpensive plastic top hats for about $1.00 each. From the audience, it looks great!

To make an inexpensive beard, take Elmer's glue and paint the boy's face where the beard will go. Take cotton balls, stretch them out, and lay them over the glue on the boy's face. Push the cotton gently with your hand to make sure it sticks. (Explain to "Abe" that the glue is going to pull on his face a little, but that it won't hurt.) Then take dark brown eye shadow and gently rub it over the cotton beard.

President George Washington

Convince your young man that all men wore tights during George Washington's era! He will need a pair of knickers and white tights as well as a ruffled lady's blouse – preferably with a high collar. Shop at a secondhand store for everything you need for this costume.

For the knickers, take a pair of dress pants and cut them off below the knee. If you are good with a needle and thread, make a casing for elastic (for a nice finish) or use iron-on hemming tape to keep the edges from fraying. A lady's ruffled blouse will be easy to access. However, a jacket with tails might be impossible. In case you can't find one with tails, settle for a solid colored jacket and hem the sleeves to the correct length. Then go to a fabric store and buy one yard of gold fringe. With a needle and thread, sew the gold fringe on the shoulders of the jacket in a loop across the shoulder. This will look like the epaulettes on an officer's jacket. Also, "George" needs a neutral colored vest to go with his outfit. Finally, if you can find a tricorn hat (with the brim turned up into three peaks) the outfit will be complete.

George Washington would not be complete without a powdered wig! They are quite costly in the theatrical supply catalogs but you can create one with some effort. Take a pair of panty hose and cut all but 3" of the legs off. Place the waist of the panty hose over the bottom of a medium size mixing bowl (or a wig head, if you are so lucky to have one). This serves as a base for the powdered wig. Tie a rubber band around the leg stumps. With a needle and thread, sew the leg stubs to the "head" of the wig. Purchase polyester quilting batting (available at any craft or fabric store) and cut into strips 2' long and 2" wide. Sew the strips of batting to the front of the waistband of the pantyhose. Bring all the strips together in the back for a low ponytail. Cover the rubber band with a black ribbon, and you have an inexpensive powdered wig!

Here is a picture of my son, Mark, as a 2nd grader playing the part of "George Washington." He is wearing a powdered wig I give directions to make. The curls are just a pink sponge curler, wrapped in white yarn. He is wearing a tuxedo jacket I got from a secondhand store. It was too big for him but the length was what I wanted. I hemmed the sleeves and added gold ribbon on the cuffs and over the buttons. Notice the buckles on his shoes. They are made of cardboard covered with aluminum foil and hot glued in place.

Snowmen

To make a snowman, start with two large white garbage bags. Cut a hole in the top of one for the head and two smaller holes on the sides for the arms. Cut two larger holes in the top of the other bag for the leg holes. Have the child dress in a white sweat suit. Then have the child step into the bottom trash bag. Use crumpled-up newspaper to stuff the bag around the child. Use masking tape (preferably white) and tape the open end of the garbage bag around the waist of the child. Take the other bag and place it on the child. Again, stuff crumpled newspaper around the child and use the masking tape to secure the bag to the child's waist. Before taping the bag to the child, you might want to wrap some ballerina netting to the outside of the newspaper, to soften the shape of the snowman and to keep the newspaper from showing through the white garbage bag. Tape a few 4-inch black circles cut from construction paper. Add a scarf and top hat to complete the outfit.

You can outfit your larger kids as snowmen. White sweat pants look great! The girl on the left is wearing white tights. I added a variety of hats and scarves on the snowmen for color and contrast. Their faces are painted with white clown makeup. The bodies are stuffed with newspaper. Add a layer of ballerina netting between the newspaper and costume if the newspaper shows through.

Nuts

THE BASICS

All nuts will need either dark tights or sweat pants dyed to the appropriate color. Some type of long sleeved shirt should be worn under the costume. To make the nut body, use small garbage bags, with drawstrings. Cut openings in

Featured in
Nuts
Musical by
John Jacobson &
John Higgins

the bottom of the bag for the child's legs, cut openings in the sides for the child's arms and then stuff newspaper between the child and the garbage bags. Pull the drawstring up around the child's neck to secure it.

SPECIALTIES

Acorns: Use brown garbage bags and cut openings in the bag, following the directions above. Stuff a lot of newspaper in the bottom of the acorn, than in the top, to give it an "acorn" shape. Add a brown beret, or improvise with brown felt for the hat.

Brazil Nuts: Same as acorns but add a colored ruffle out of crepe paper to the top of the garbage bags. Add colored ruffles to the sleeve of the shirt. Instead of a brown beret, attach some plastic fruit to a hair band – Carmen Miranda style!

Cashew: (a-chew!) Same as acorn but add a bathrobe, slippers and a sleep cap. Bring a box of tissues.

Chestnut: A muscleman outfit, or put gym shorts over costume.

Peanut: Take quilt batting and wrap it around the child several times, cutting holes for the arms. Keep wrapping until it is about 6" thick around the child's body. Take jute and wrap the child's torso several times, vertically and horizontally. This will give a checkerboard look that peanuts have. Use brown floral spray and spray the outer layer of quilt batting.

Pine Nut: Same as acorn but add a green cap.

Pistachio: Needs to be green, so find green tights and use a white garbage bag and spray paint green. Add a green hat.

Costumes Through the Ages

The Roman Empire

The toga is a universal symbol for the Roman Empire. A white bed sheet will work perfectly. The easiest way to tie a toga is to fold the sheet in half and place on one side of the body, under the arm. Take the front half and wrap around to the back. Take the back and wrap it around the front. Tie above the shoulder. I always insist that my students wear a swimsuit under the toga, to keep from shocking the audience if the knot comes loose! Sandals with lots of laces were also worn then. A cheap alternative to a Roman sandal would be take a pair of cheap flip flops and spray paint them brown. Take two one-yard lengths of gross-grain ribbon (sold at craft shops) and tie on the flip flop. Place the flip flop on the foot and tie the ribbons around the ankle.

The Middle Ages

Convince your young lads (and their fathers!) that all lads in the Middle Ages wore tights. (I have had boys drop out of a production because they found out they had to wear tights!) The boys are the easy ones to outfit for the Middle Ages. A trip to the local secondhand shop will give you everything you need. Tunics and tights are what the men wore with belts or scarves tied loosely around the waist. Take a man's dress shirt and wash it before you alter it. (If you wash it afterwards, it will unravel and ruin the costume.) Every man's dress shirt that has a collar also has a collar band. Simply cut off the collar and leave the collar band on. Put the belt on the boy before you mark the hem length. Always make it longer than you think necessary because the audience might be looking up from the front rows.

Another look to give some variety are women's blouses from the 1980s that have a high ruffled collar. A trip to the local secondhand shop will provide you lots of blouses. Any color will do. The satins and silks that the blouses are made of will present well on stage. Take two yards of cheap fabric and fold it in half. Cut an 11-inch slit in the center of the fold for the neck to go through. If it's too big, pin the extra with safety pins. Leave a 12-inch opening on the sides, then sew or hot glue the sides. These openings are for the arms. Again, make it plenty long. Loosely tie a belt or sash around the waist.

Hats that were worn were berets or a Robin Hood-type hat.

The young man is wearing a woman's tunic that is too big for him, purchased at a secondhand store. A gold cord serves as a belt. I found the beret and ostrich feather in some old band uniforms that had been discarded. Some feathers and "jewels" glued on the beret make a nice finish.

These "guards" are wearing matching women's tunics with an overlay cut out of felt. Directions are given. The hats are margarine tubs painted gold with ostrich feather hot glued on. Holes punched in the sides hold the ¼ " elastic braid. The plastic swords came from a party store. Glue a few jewels on the swords and they look much more royal!

Someone might have to sew to create the female costumes from the Middle Ages. The ladies wore layers of dresses. It started with something like a nightgown but was very plain and floor length. Over that was worn a loose shift, similar to an apron but it had a front and a back. You could create this with a minor amount of sewing. Take enough fabric to go twice the length of the girl or woman from shoulder to floor. Add about six inches to this length. Fold in half and cut a semi-circle from the fold about 12 inches wide and 6 inches deep (smaller if you are making one for a child). Then, keep it folded in half and cut out a large semi-circle from the two sides. Make it about 18 inches long and 6 inches wide. From there, sew the side seams together or simply hot glue them. Drape this over the girl and hem to the correct length. This goes over the bottom night gown dress. Add a belt or purse across the chest.

Renaissance (1450-1600)

For the female Renaissance costume, scour the local secondhand shop or send home a note asking for donations. The prom dresses from the 1970s and 1980s make great Renaissance costumes. A leg-of-mutton sleeve on an old prom dress or bridesmaid's dress is perfect! The dropped waist line of the '80s is wonderful too! If the majority of dresses are this type, you could add a few dresses with the long sleeves that are noted for being worn during this period. The prom dresses from the past few years that have the camisole with the toile skirt will do nicely here as well!

Hats are a necessary item for women. The simplest way to make a Renaissance hat is to purchase a small metal ring that is about 4" or 6". (Craft shops sell them.) Buy one yard of chiffon or some other sheer fabric and gather one end up with your fingers to about 3 inches. Run it through the ring and pull out about 3 inches. Hot glue this to the longer piece. You can hot glue a hair comb or simply buy hair clips to hold it on the head. Cone hats (similar to a witch hat) made out of construction paper and covered with fabric look great from the stage. Attach a sheer piece of fabric to the pointed end of the cone. You can hold the hat in place by attaching quarter-inch elastic to the hat.

For the guys, again, it's tunics and tights! The tunics during the Renaissance were much more elaborate than those during the Middle Ages. Again, a trip to a secondhand store should yield what you are looking for. Look for a woman's jacket that buttons all the way up. If it is too short, you could layer a tunic under it to make it the appropriate length. Look for jackets that have heavy embroidery, jewels, and large buttons and embellishments. The women's clothes of the 1990's would be very appropriate. Satin, silk, velvet, etc... these are the fabrics that will present well for the Renaissance. A ruffled collar and a cape will set the costume off.

Hats worn are berets and pill box hats. You can take a plain basic beret and turn it into a wonderful accessory by hot gluing a few "jewels" and feathers on it. You will find both in craft stores. You can take a large butter tub, spray paint it and it becomes the base for a wonderful hat. Punch two holes on the side near the top to run quarter-inch elastic to hold the cap in place under the chin. Glue "jewels" or feathers on the painted butter tub. If you could find some ostrich feathers or peacock feathers, it would really be grand!

This shows a simple "pillow case" tunic and matching beret I made out of striped fabric. The old silk blouse was purchased at a secondhand store.

17th and 18th Centuries (1600s & 1700s)

The men are finally wearing pants or knickers!! (Maybe you won't lose any boys during this time period.) Knickers are very simple to make. Ask the boys to bring you a pair of dress pants or khakis that are too short for them. You simply cut them off below the knee. If you have someone who can sew, they can sew a casing and run elastic through it or they can just be worn below the knee. If your boys don't have any dress pants that are too small, visit a secondhand store and buy them for a couple of dollars a pair. Everything you need for this costume can come from a secondhand store, except the tights. Tights are a *must*, but hopefully the guys won't resist too much since they will be wearing them under knickers. (You can buy tights online any time of the year. I found a website that sells 6X tights that fit my heaviest high school boy, for about $6.00 a pair.) Black shoes can be embellished with buckles made out of cardboard covered with aluminum foil. Look for men's suit jackets that are a little longer than normal. Put a woman's ruffled blouse on the guy, add a vest, the jacket, knickers and you have the complete outfit. A woman's curly wig (any color will do) pulled back into a pony tail will complete the outfit.

The guys are wearing dress jackets that I purchased at a secondhand store. Ladies wigs, knickers and dark stockings finish each costume.

For the girls, almost anything that is long and full will work. Scour secondhand stores for old prom dresses and even look for hoop skirts or crinolines. I have found that even the most humble costume takes on a new appeal with a hoop skirt or crinoline under it. The girls' hair must be put up, preferably with ringlets and curls. Big hats, or Martha Washington hats will finish off this costume.

Here is another Gunne Sax prom dress with a 2nd hand straw hat that I hot glued silk flower and ribbons on. Notice the young man's knickers, plaid vest and wig – all purchased from a secondhand store.

Nineteenth Century (1800s)

Your boys will be glad to know that stockings and knickers have now been replaced with pants – real pants!! Men wore long pants, vests, long jackets, and bow ties in the 19th Century. Top hats and lower hats were also worn. You can find what you need in a secondhand store. Solid jackets and vests can be purchased quite inexpensively. If you wanted to buy some crepe hair from a theatrical online catalog and make some mustaches and mutton chops, that would be fantastic. You will need to purchase Liquid Latex to hold the crepe hair to the face. Both are sold at the same place.

For the ladies, again, go shopping at a secondhand store. Keep an eye out for hoop slips or crinolines. Long dresses with lots of ruffles were very popular. Old prom dresses will work great. The women didn't wear strapless gowns like they do today, so you might want to add a shawl or a short jacket over the gown. Hair must be put up.

Twentieth Century (1900s)

The little girls are wearing below-the-knee 2nd hand dresses with stockings and ribbons in their hair. The "ladies" are wearing long 2nd hand dresses and hats. Refer to directions on how to make the plastic skimmer hats look real. All the young men are wearing secondhand men's sport jackets.

The men's clothes hasn't change much from the last century. Ascots and ribbon ties are still around. The basic suit will work great. Add a vest but keep the coat buttoned. The boater hat can be purchased at any party store. Look for the white plastic hat with a red, white and blue paper band in the Patriotic section. Take that plastic hat and carefully remove the paper band. Paint the hat using a flat spray paint. Off white, beige, grey or tan are the colors you want to use. Then take the paper band and use it as a pattern to cut another band out of felt. (Use felt so it doesn't ravel.) Cutting a straight band will not work. There is a curve to the band and if you don't use their band as a pattern, your new band will not lay correctly. Do not try to hot glue the band on the hat because it will melt the hat. Use Elmer's glue and let it dry overnight. With the flat paint and a real fabric band, the hat looks real!

Women's clothing is finally changing. The dresses are narrower but still long. Big hats are very popular. You can take a straw hat from a secondhand store and decorate it with netting or flowers and turn a plain hat into a fashion statement.

The "Roaring Twenties"

The men's clothing still hasn't changed much. Pants are baggier and plaids are everywhere. Bow ties are very popular. You can create bow ties with ribbon by simply creating a flat bow and hot gluing it on a long ribbon. Attach Velcro to both ends of the ribbon that you have measured to make sure it fits the boy's neck. Plaid suits are easy to find in secondhand stores. The boater hats from the last section work real well in this era, as does the fedora. Good luck on finding real fedoras in a secondhand store! You can buy plastic ones at party supply stores, but they don't hold up very well.

This flapper girl's dress came straight from a secondhand store. The jacket is too long for the boy, but that was the look I wanted. Use iron-on hemming tape to make the sleeves the correct length. Look for fedoras at yard sales.

The women are finally showing some leg! The dresses are straight. You can look in a secondhand store and find variations of the flapper dress. You can take a plain straight shift and hot glue fringe onto the dress to make a flapper dress. Buy 1-inch stretch sequin braid and hot glue some tall feathers on the front of the braid and place on the girl's head. Add a few strands of long beads and she's ready for the "Charleston"!!

1930s and 1940s

The man's suit is perfect for this era with a real loud and tacky neck tie. Plaids and solids for jackets and pants were what men worn then. A visit to the secondhand store will provide you everything you need. Look for dress pants that are a bit too big. You can hem them to the correct length using an iron-on hemming tape (found in fabric stores). If your boys don't have dress shirts and ties, the store should have plenty. Also look for pairs of black dress shoes. Using white enamel hobby paint, paint the shoes to look like two-tone "wing tips." Keep a look-out for a real fedora. Sometimes yard sales are where you can find fedoras. (I found an estate sale once with 25 fedoras. I bought them for $3.00 each!)

The dresses that were fashionable in the 80s and early 90s are perfect for this era. The secondhand stores are full of these type dresses with the big shoulder pads and dropped waists, just like the women wore back then. If the dress is too big, take it up under the arms. Hem the length to mid-calf. Have them wear a pair of pantyhose, and with a black eyeliner pencil, draw a line down the back of the leg. This will make them look like the old time seamed stockings. Add a pair of clunky shoes and an "old lady" church hat, and she's ready to swing!

In these next pictures, all the girls are wearing 80's dresses with the big shoulder pads there were purchased at a secondhand store. Add a hat and it works! All the guys are wearing secondhand jackets with their own dress pants. I picked up neck ties and hats at a secondhand store.

Here I painted part of the shoes on the right with white paint to make them two-toned.

This photo shows how I used old band uniforms for a "Save-A-Soul" mission. Adding black skirts for the girls takes the band uniform look away. This type band uniform also works well for toy soldiers in a Christmas play.

1950s

Suits are still real popular but now, branch out and have the boys wear tight pants and roll up the pants legs to show white socks with their penny loafers. A plain white tee shirt is all he needs besides a leather jacket.

For the girls, you don't have to have a poodle skirt although that would be nice. Any skirt that is full is great. If you could find an old square dance costume and take the short crinoline to put under the skirt, it would be great! Blouses are white with a rounded collar. Make sure the girls have bright red lipstick on and lots of blush. Don't forget a ponytail with a big bow. Dresses for the women are much like the dresses from the '40s. Secondhand stores are full of dresses that will do.

Underwater Creatures

Fish

Fish costumes are not as easy to create. Here's what I do. Round up some large black lights. Take a 4-foot florescent light fixture and have a plug wired to it. Paint the fixture black and lay it on the stage. You can purchase 4-foot black lights at hardware stores very inexpensively. Make huge fish out of cardboard – I use an entire 4'x8' piece of cardboard. Paint them with florescent paint, and then cut them out. Put the "fish" in black sweat suits. The "fish" come out, say their lines and everyone smiles. At a certain point, turn off the stage lights and turn on the black lights. You will hear the audience actually gasp. The effect is stunning. Have your "fish" move as though they are swimming. Your audience will walk away remembering nothing else!

Lobsters and Crabs

Dress the child in a bright red sweat suit. You will need six red socks for the crab legs. Stuff the socks with polyfill. Stuff two of the socks all the way out, two about midway and two quite short. (You don't want all the legs the same length.) Starting with the longest sock at the top and the shortest on the bottom, sew three of the socks on the side seam of the sweat suit and the other three on the other side. Make sure the longest are at the top and the shortest are at the bottom. With a needle and a thread, run fishing line through the end of the bottom "leg" and tie a knot on the top of the sock, making the fishing line secure. Go through the next leg and tie a knot at the top and bottom of the sock, leaving about four inches between the two legs. Go through the top sock and again, leave a 4-inch space and secure it with fishing line. Take the fishing line and tie it to the underside of the sleeve of the sweat suit. Cut two sets of mittens out of black felt and hot glue the edges together. Make them much larger than the child's hands. Stuff the "claws" with polyfill but leave enough space for the child to put his hand inside the "claw". Safety pin the "claw" to the wrist cuff of the sweat suit. Some red face paint with big black circles around the eyes will dazzle the audience!

Mermaids

A mermaid needs to start with a two-piece swimsuit. Make sure she doesn't mind showing her midriff. Take inexpensive green fabric (or dye an old white sheet green) and cut into 12-inch strips. Wrap the strips around her hips and down her legs. Leave enough slack so she can walk. Take a measurement from below her knee to the floor and add 12 inches. Use that measurement and cut strips that length. Safety pin these strips to the wrapped costume, just below her knee. (Make sure she goes to the bathroom before you wrap her up!) Pin these strips all the way around her wrapped legs. Add a seashell necklace and you have a beautiful Mermaid!

Sharks

Take a basic grey sweat suit and purchase a grey baseball cap. If you can't find the color you need, dye a white one. You will need grey foam sheets and white foam sheets. Cut a large "dorsal" fin out of the grey foam sheet and hot glue on the back of the sweat shirt. Cut large triangle teeth out of the white foam sheets and glue them to the bib of the baseball cap. Pull the cap way down on the child's face, so you can't really see his face.

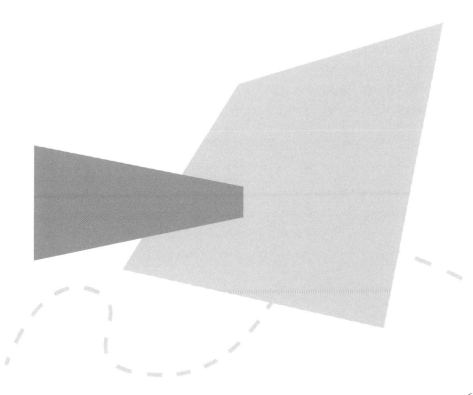

About the Writer

Janet Edewaard received her Bachelor of Science Degree from Florida State University. Having taught many areas of the Arts, including Band, Choir, Art, Elementary Music, and Drama, Janet has written costume suggestions for some of Hal Leonard's best-selling children's musicals.

Janet currently teaches Middle School and High School Choir and Art in her hometown of Blountstown, Florida, where her roots reach back many generations. Janet is an active member of the Florida Vocal Association and the American Choral Directors Association. She serves as the Middle School Repertoire and Standards Chair for the Florida ACDA and serves as the coordinator for the ACDA Florida Male Honor Choir.

In the summer, she is fondly known as Miss Janet, the swimming lessons teacher. Over the past 25 summers, thousands of children have learned to swim in her backyard. Janet is married to Bruce Edewaard and they have a blended family of seven children and two beautiful grandchildren!